YOUR KNOWLEDGE HAS VALUE

- We will publish your bachelor's and master's thesis, essays and papers

- Your own eBook and book - sold worldwide in all relevant shops

- Earn money with each sale

Upload your text at www.GRIN.com
and publish for free

Bibliographic information published by the German National Library:

The German National Library lists this publication in the National Bibliography; detailed bibliographic data are available on the Internet at http://dnb.dnb.de .

This book is copyright material and must not be copied, reproduced, transferred, distributed, leased, licensed or publicly performed or used in any way except as specifically permitted in writing by the publishers, as allowed under the terms and conditions under which it was purchased or as strictly permitted by applicable copyright law. Any unauthorized distribution or use of this text may be a direct infringement of the author s and publisher s rights and those responsible may be liable in law accordingly.

Imprint:

Copyright © 2016 GRIN Verlag, Open Publishing GmbH
Print and binding: Books on Demand GmbH, Norderstedt Germany
ISBN: 9783668430587

This book at GRIN:

http://www.grin.com/en/e-book/356882/guinness-s-impact-on-irish-culture

Abigail Randow

Guinness's Impact on Irish Culture

GRIN Publishing

GRIN - Your knowledge has value

Since its foundation in 1998, GRIN has specialized in publishing academic texts by students, college teachers and other academics as e-book and printed book. The website www.grin.com is an ideal platform for presenting term papers, final papers, scientific essays, dissertations and specialist books.

Visit us on the internet:

http://www.grin.com/

http://www.facebook.com/grincom

http://www.twitter.com/grin_com

Inhaltsverzeichnis

1. Sayings about Guinness® beer..4
2. Arthur Guinness: Biography..4
   2.1 Childhood and Beginnings..4
   2.2 Business Life..5
3. Influence on the life of Irish population..6
   3.1 Pub...6
   3.2 Lifestyle of the population..7
   3.3 Social aspects...8
      3.3.1 Religion...8
      3.3.2 Employees...8
      3.3.3 Charity...9
   3.4 Parliament...9
4. Influence on the world...10
   4.1 Guinness® World Records...10
   4.2 Consumption worldwide...11
5. Conclusion..12

1. Sayings about Guinness® beer

Nowadays the word *Guinness* or rather the beer is a common word and product and stands for one of the largest breweries in the world. Over ten Million pints Guinness® a day are sold worldwide. Not only in Ireland, where it evolved, but also in the rest of the world, the slogans such as *Guinness is good for you* and *My Goodness, My Guinness* are widespread and probably often used as an excuse to drink a lot of beer. In the Irish culture, there are many sayings about alcohol and especially about beer. A lot of times there are toasts like "Here's to a long life and a merry one. A quick death and an easy one. A pretty girl and an honest one. A cold beer and another one! " [1] Even Peter O´Toole, a famous Irish actor said: "My favorite food from my homeland is Guinness. My second choice is Guinness. My third choice - would have to be Guinness."[2]

These sayings wouldn´t have been that famous and important, if Guinness hadn´t been so successful with his beer and if he hadn´t been after the idea of bringing beer closer to the population as an alternative to whiskey and other strong drinks.

But how did he get this brewery to evolve from a small local business to one of the most successful in the world and how did a seemingly ordinary beer have so much influence on Ireland and later on the world?

2. Arthur Guinness: Biography
2.1 Childhood and Beginnings

At the time Arthur was born, to the begin of the 18th century, it was very common for families to brew their own ale due to the uncleanliness of the water. The proletariat could mostly only afford whiskey or homemade poteen, which led to a lot of drunkenness among the Irish. Arthurs Grandfather started brewing ale (historically, the term referred to a drink brewed without hops)[3] in his family and even bought a license for selling it. For the family, it was better than whiskey because children are unable to process alcohol. The low- alcohol ale could be stored for a short time, as the alcohol killed any germs. „Brewing ale was [also] an ancient Irish skill, improved by the later addition of hops. " [4]

---

[1] Popik, Barry. "Here´s to a long life and a merry one… (toast)". *The Big Apple*. Barry Popik. n.d. Web. 01.11.2016.

[2] BrainyQuote. „Peter O´Toole Quotes ". *BrainyQuotes*. BrainyQuotes. 2001- 2016. Web. 01.11.2016.

[3] Bendbrewfest. "About Ales" *BEND BREWFEST.* BEND BREWFEST. 2016. N.d. Web. 22.03.2016.

[4] Guinness, Patrick. *Arthur´s Round: The life and times of brewing legend Arthur Guinness*. (London: Peter Owen, 2008) (whole paragraph). 19.

Arthur was born around the 24th of September 1725 in Celbridge, Ireland, where he also grew up. His parents Elisabeth Read (whose father brewed ale and where she also learned that skill and passed it onto her children) and Richard Guinness were normal, hardworking people who tried to provide the best future for their three children. Arthurs father worked for the protestant dean of Kildare and earned a good amount of money to support the family. As Arthur got older he helped with the book keeping and was also his Registrar. That´s how he probably had access to a library where he could read which helped him shape his mind for understanding the wider world. [5]

There were several family links in the Dublin commercial world, to whom they only needed less than a day´s travel from his hometown. Those connections were maintained by his father whenever he was in Dublin. Compared with the most of the rural Irish people, the contacts to the city gave Arthur another unusual advantage.

As mentioned before, a lot of ale was brewed in the household of the Guinness's, and so Arthur also took up these skills. Between 1752 and 1755 he also helped out brewing in the inn of his father´s second wife. He enjoyed working there and thought about the aspect to maybe someday open his own brewery since he had a talent for brewing and already knew then, that he wanted to help people. [6]

> Beer had taken almost a moral quality of its own at this time. Starting in London, where many of the very poor had become dangerously addicted to cheap gin, a mixture of tax policy and encouragement in the 1740s had led to beer being seen as the weaker, healthier, safer alternative. [...] The underlying message supported Arthur throughout his career.[7]

2.2 Business Life

Most of the people know the story of Arthur leasing the St. James Brewery for 9000 years, with an annual cost of only forty- five pounds. But only few have heard about the long journey before his most famous highlight of his work. At the time his big project launched in 1759, he was already thirty- four years old. Before that, he grew hops as a young man and so it seems likely that he therefore also brewed ale, helping his mother in their home in Celbridge. [8] As already mentioned, he helped in the background of the White Hart Inn of Richard Guinness' second wife and with thirty years, in 1755 he took on a brewery in Leixlip, about eleven miles west from Dublin. [9]

1799 he stopped brewing ale, started brewing porter and concentrated on improving his beer creation that developed from the porter beer.

---
[5] Guinness, Patrick. (whole paragraph). 31ff.
[6] Guinness, Patrick. (whole paragraph). 53f.
[7] Guinness, Patrick. 54.
[8] Guinness, Patrick. (whole paragraph). 43 + 45.
[9] Guinness, Patrick. (whole paragraph). 53 + 59.

He copied this dark style of beer that developed from well- hopped beers made from brown malt, but more improved. Arthur had invented a special brewer´s yeast, that was nicknamed *God – is – good* because it grows in the progress, can be skimmed off and be used over and over again. Guinness took this special yeast and copied the porter with this ingredient. That was so delicious and special that most of the people said that he copied porter, only better. [10]

3. Influence on the life of Irish population
3.1 Pub

In 1791 the parliament increased the cost of the liquor licenses, so the smaller and poorer publicans couldn´t brew homemade poteen, which was untaxable and often badly made. The then remaining brewers had one main worry because the beer imports from England were increasing more and more. Also, those tax- paying brewers were in competition with the local distillers and poteen- makers across the island, because they were under- taxed and therefor had lower production costs. On the 14th of February in 1792 Arthur Guinness once again went to the parliamentary committee, so they checked, if the regulations, that less strong liquor had been sold and drunk, Guinness had initiated before had the wanted effect. This led to the *1792 Act*. Here the fines for infringements were raised and workmen´s wages could no longer be paid in a pub or in liquor, so there was an improvement in this issue. Also, the parliament said, that the poor had to be protected from themselves. This reduction on beer tax effected, that brewers used more hops and malt wouldn´t have to be so expensive and poor people didn´t need to drink whiskey and other strong liquor. [11]

Three years later, in 1795, the parliament revoked all taxes on beer. Because of this triumph the most famous brewers´ supporter, Henry Grattan, wrote a letter to the Dublin brewers: "It is at your source that Parliament will find in its own country the means of health with all her flourishing consequences, and the cure of intoxication with all her misery" [12]. Because Guinness respected Grattan very much, he thought what was good for Grattan, would be good for Ireland. The imports from England decreased by 65 000 barrels per years in a time range of ten years. Furthermore, the prime minister at that time abolished tollages into England, to support the Irish export trade. Around this time, in 1794, Guinness´s porter was mentioned the first time in a magazine. [13]

In 1900 Guinness® tried new barley and because it would have taken a huge effort to grow new grain and through the time gap between growing it, the weather

---
[10] Guinness, Patrick. (whole paragraph). 60ff.
[11] Guinness, Patrick. (whole paragraph). 164- 166.
[12] Lynch, Patrick and Vaizey, John. *Guinness´s Brewery in the Irish Economy 1759-1876*. (New York: Cambridge University Press, 1960) p. 58.
[13] Guinness, Patrick. (whole paragraph). 167f.

would have been to different, a new brewer was recruited. It was the mathematically minded Englishman William Sealy Gosset. He invented a statistical way of interpreting the results that are produced from small samples so it didn´t needed to be produced in a great amount. Gosset published his technique in an international journal under the pseudonym *Student*. This technique, called 'Student's t-test', is still widely used by statisticians. "By helping to improve the quality of the barley and the brew, Gosset's test helped to establish Guinness® as a reliable, quality brand." [14]

Nowadays you can find Guinness® Extra Stout - the beer Arthur Guinness invented at that time - in every Irish pub. If an Irish person is asked what they think about Guinness®, I think you almost never hear somebody say, they don´t like it. People all around the world consider Guinness® typical Irish. Peter Riegert, an American actor and scriptwriter even put it like this that he likes Guinness® and that by liking it you could say that this would make everyone Irish. [15]

3.2 Lifestyle of the population
Guinness® got more and more popular, all around Ireland. Through the abolished taxes, more people could afford beer and through the improvements mentioned before of the statistics they also wanted to drink more beer. The slogan *Guinness is good for you* came to the fore because the population realized that whiskey and gin couldn´t possibly be healthy nor supportive for one's health. Due to the very rich taste of the Guinness® beer you can´t drink that much, because you very quickly get a stuffed feeling. Robbie Williams, a British musician, once said "I've been watching what I eat. When I was putting on all the weight, I was drinking Guinness® and not eating. I didn't have room to because I was drinking all the time."[16] This was very practical back then because the people wanted to drink Guinness® but didn´t get very drunk. Also, there aren´t as much calories in it and nowadays it is declared typical Irish all around the world.

Going to pubs is also considered very typical for Ireland and has been enjoyed for a very long time. In the past it was normal that beer was sold to the pubs directly in barrels to sell to the population and not in bottles or cans to the consumer himself. So, through the good Guinness® taste, the people wanted to drink it but only could buy it in pubs and it developed that they went there very regularly. Nowadays the Irish pub is sometimes also called *The extended living room* because people go there so often and also because of its nice and homelike atmosphere. As no one knows where the pubs originated from, it seems as if they were always there and as already pointed out, inns were a form of a pub where Arthur also already helped along. Even though the combination of pub and music developed as recently as around the 1960s, it´s still considered typical and full of tradition.

---

[14] Mary. "How statistics helped to make Guinness good!". *Ingenious Ireland*. Heidi Jermyn. 25.09.2012. Web. 06.09.2016.
[15] BrainyQuote. „Peter Riegert Quotes ". *BrainyQuotes*. BrainyQuotes. 2001- 2016. Web. 02.11.2016.
[16] BrainyQuote. „Robbie Williams Quotes ". *BrainyQuotes*. BrainyQuotes. 2001- 2016. Web. 02.11.2016.

3.3 Social aspects

Arthur was ahead for his times, considering the working condition, religious freedom and helping the less fortunate, even though he himself was very wealthy. He brought his ideas to his children and taught them his values and opinions.

In the 1760s he joined a movement named *Kildare Knot*, a relatively exclusive club, that wanted to ban dueling in Ireland. Arthur Young blamed these typical duels on excessive drinking in 1786 by the small, poor people, who "Hunt in the day, get drunk in the evening and fight the next morning" [17] This statement also could have influenced Guinness. [18]

3.3.1 Religion

Around 1773 he was the Treasurer and later on the governor of the *Meath Hospital* and that added to his social respectability. In his position, he really made sure that it provided good care for the poor and that all people, no matter what religion could stay there and get free medical aid. He also gave money to a lot of other charities. [19]

Furthermore, he took part in the *Sunday School movement*, that tried to provide basic education for children. Arthur Guinness looked further, because for him that was a part of reformation in prison matters. He believed that normal education combined with teaching the bible would keep people from sliding in a life of crime. [20]

Nowadays we still notice the things he tried to improve in his times. Arthur was a protestant, but described as a person who was very open to the Catholics. Guinness influenced the parliament as he always stated his opinion positively towards Catholics. In 1793 the Catholics could even vote the first time since 1728. As a very respected nobleman and brewer the people listened to him and thought about him and his words. He was publicly in favor of full equalization and emphasized that everybody is the same and that there are no inherent differences.[21] Even though years later this regulation was destructed, his ideas lived on. In his business, he had no problem employing Catholics and that was carried on by mostly all heads of the brewery until this day.

3.3.2 Employees

Due to his involvement with the care for the poor it´s no wonder that he also wanted his workers to have good working conditions and always did his best to help improve these. His opinions and improvements survived long after his death. In the 19th and 20th centuries the Guinness® board members provided benefits for its

---

[17] Guinness, Patrick. 125.
[18] Guinness, Patrick. (whole paragraph). 121ff.
[19] Christian Worldview Journal (ed.). „Christians who changed their world ". *Colsoncenter, Breakpoint.* Christian Worldview Journal. N.d. Web. 06.09.2016. (whole paragraph).
[20] Christian Worldview Journal (ed.). „Christians who changed their world ". *Colsoncenter, Breakpoint.* Christian Worldview Journal. N.d. Web. 06.09.2016. (whole paragraph).
[21] Guinness, Patrick. 181ff.

employees that were one of a kind in Ireland at that time. Workers received health insurance, subsidized meals, pensions, 20% higher wages than the average worker at that time, and since 1872 housings near to the brewery. [22]

In 1890 the *Iveagh Trust* was founded, that provided shelters for the poor in London and Dublin. Additionally, they received three meals a day, a coupon for two pints beer or a token for goods in the *Co- operative- store.* For married couples with small children there were free, little bottles of Guinness® with yeast rich in vitamin B for a better nutrition. At the beginning of the twentieth century more support for Guinness® employees came along, for example they received gratis train tickets for travelling to the countryside. [23]

3.3.3 Charity

A further example in more recent history is the fact that the Guinness® brewery still wanted a good relationship with the Britain's and wanted to help people in need. Every British soldier serving World War II received a bottle of Guinness® beer for their Christmas dinner. [24]

Due to the very high need of water in the beer production, Guinness® watched their production very carefully and managed to save six billion liters of water and wanted to provide Africa with clean drinking water. So, in 2007 the *Water of Life* program was founded and since then they worked together with other organizations to support necessary arrangements, like filter systems for the own home. Since the beginning of this program they operated two hundred projects in eighteen countries to provide clean water for ten Million people. [25]

In 2009, the *Arthur Guinness Fund* (AGF) is established. It developed in the course of the 250 years anniversary of the brewery. The fund is administrated by the *Guinness & Co.*, the brewery´s head. It provides two and a half Million Euros to support social corporations in Ireland. [26] This is another great example of how the importance of having a good influence on society still has got a big impact on the brewery. Arthurs values are still respected and are tried to be continued.

3.4 Parliament

As already pointed out, Arthur was very present in the parliament and tried to change the social situation in Ireland and the relationship to Britain. In his opinion around 1785 "social changes in Ireland were […] necessary, but a link to Britain

---

[22] Micah White. "Hops to it! 7 Facts on Beer Mastermind Arthur Guinness". *Biography.* A&E Television Networks, LLC. 17.03.2015. Web. 06.09.2016. (whole paragraph).
[23] Guinnes.com. „Unsere Geschichte ". *Guinness.com.* Guinness & Co. 2016. Web. 04.11.2016. (whole paragraph).
[24] Tim Challies. "The Philanthropists: Arthur Guinness". *challis.com.* Tim Challies. 24.11.2013. Web. 06.09.2016. (whole paragraph).
[25] Guinnes.com. „Unsere Geschichte". *Guinness.com.* Guinness & Co. 2016. Web. 04.11.2016. (whole paragraph).
[26] Guinnes.com. „Unsere Geschichte". *Guinness.com.* Guinness & Co. 2016. Web. 03.11.2016. (whole paragraph).

should remain" [27] From the 1760s until his death he was a member of *Dublin´s City Council* but it was described as a long and powerless involvement. He was very busy and couldn´t leave his business, whose money was badly needed, since he had to provide for himself, his wife and his ten children. [28] He really wanted to change the situations but hardly could make a direct difference about it, only as his legacy living on in his descendants and his business.

Some theories exist that the Irish parliament copied the Guinness® logo and turned it around. The link here is that the government wanted to use the harp, an ancient Irish symbol as its emblem for their newfound independence in 1922. But because Guinness® already had introduced the harp symbol as a distinctive mark in 1862[29] they had to turn it around. The logo itself already appeared a long time ago and the considered typical Irish harp is based on the harp of Turlough O'Carolan, a famous harper who died in 1738. [30]

The harp is in all cases the emblem of many institutions but the most famous are pictured above. Many establishments take the instrument as their logo based on these two, which is an evidence for the status symbol of Ireland, also induced through Guinness®.

4. Influence on the world
4.1 Guinness® World Records

Arthur Guinness himself didn´t establish the *Guinness World Records*, but the Managing Director of the Guinness® Brewery in the 1950s, Sir Hugh Beaver had the idea for this book. He got the idea as he attended a shooting party in County Wexford. The hosts and him argued about which was the fastest game bird in Europe, wanted to look it up but couldn´t find it in any reference book. Four years after this argument, in 1954, he had the idea for a book, so that pub arguments could be settled easier. Sir Beaver invited the twins Norris and Ross McWhirter to compile a book where all kinds of facts and figures would be written down. On the thirtieth of November, the incorporation was officially founded in England. It took thirteen and a half ninety- hour weeks to write the book, including weekends and bank holidays. In 1955 this very first edition was published and the first impression is for 50 000 copies and by Christmas *The Guinness® Book of Records* has become a bestseller in the UK. [31] The cover featured the Guinness® logo, that was at that time almost exactly

---

[27] Guinness, Patrick. 154.
[28] Guinness, Patrick. 121.
[29] Guinnes.com. „Unsere Geschichte ". *Guinness.com*. Guinness & Co. 2016. Web. 03.11.2016.
[30] National Museum of Ireland. "O'Carolan's Harp". National Museum of Ireland. NMI. 06.2014. Web. 25.10.2016.
[31] Guinness World Records. "Our history". *Guinness World Records*. Guinness World Records. N.d. Web. 06.09.2016. (whole paragraph).

the same as the Government emblem today, only with the difference that it was turned the other way around, as it is today.

Of course, the founders didn´t know that this book would become even an all-time bestseller and a very famous brand, with offices all around the world. In 1974 The Guinness® Book of Records became the biggest-selling copyright book in history with sales to date totaling 23,950,000 copies. The 1987 edition is published in thirty- one languages and through that could have been read by more than three billion people of the world. [32]

Nowadays almost everybody has heard of the Guinness® World Records and like to read it. They find inspiration, things to laugh about but also interesting facts that can be shared.

4.2 Consumption worldwide

The consumption of Guinness® is very high, over ten Million pints Guinness® a day are sold worldwide[33], two billion pints per year in over 150 countries.[34] Exportation started with England in 1796 because it was near and porter beer was already popular back then. Around 1858 most of the Irish brewers were satisfied with sales in the inland, but not Guinness®. It´s already exported all the way to New Zealand. Until 1963 every beer, also those that were going to be exported, was brewed at the St. James Gate Brewery until the company opened a new brewery in Nigeria, [35] so that the people probably needn´t to pay that much through export costs and production costs could be lowered.

In the early 1990s the sales in the inlands stagnated, so Guinness® authorized Noel Derby, the marketing director of the *Irish Pub Company* (IPCo), who deals with globalization to find a way to get the export going. The idea was – since Guinness® is broadly consumed and sold in Irish pubs – to simply export the concept of the typical Irish pub. Mel McNally was instructed to look what makes a pub typical Irish. He travelled around the whole country and gathered together the essential aspects of every good pub. Along various other things, one important point was to serve Guinness® as the most typical Irish beer. [36]

Nowadays there are a lot of Irish pubs, all around the globe. A pub operator from North Carolina said. "Irish pubs still live up to their 'Publican' roots. It gives people a place to meet, socialize and converse. It's a place of friendliness and

---

[32] Guinness World Records. "Our history". *Guinness World Records*. Guinness World Records. N.d. Web. 06.09.2016. (whole paragraph).

[33] IrishCentral Staff Writers. "Top ten facts about Guinness". *IrishCentral*. IrishCentral LLC. 01.07.2016. Web. 07.09.2016.

[34] Diageo.com. „Guinness ". *Diageo*. Diageo 2016. N.d. Web. 04.11.2016.

[35] Guinnes.com. „Unsere Geschichte". *Guinness.com*. Guinness & Co. 2016. Web. 03.11.2016.

[36] Verg, Martin. "Atmosphäre nach Maß". *GEO Special* 2 (April/ May 2007): 70. Print. (whole paragraph).

comfort. Sometimes that is what people need when times get tough." [37] A lot of people really enjoy the Irish lifestyle and those pubs are a gathering point for all people of all classes and jobs. As already mentioned, the Irish pub is sometimes also called *The extended Irish living room* because it has such a nice and homelike atmosphere.

And for all pubs, Guinness® is an essential part of their establishment because drinking alcohol is a relatively important part for the Irish culture. Some pub owners even have more alcohol sales than food sales. "[…] I don't know how restaurants with high food sales and low alcohol sales survive" [38], an owner in Kansas even said. Many people travelling to Ireland have the plan to go to a typical Irish pub and to drink a good pint of Guinness® or a glass of Jameson Irish Whiskey.

5. Conclusion

His whole life Arthur Guinness worked very hard to achieve his goals and establish his company. Even though there were many points in his life, when he could´ve thrown in the towel, he never gave up and tried more and more. He also stayed true to his intentions and values so that nobody could have gotten confused about his opinions because he always stated them clear. Guinness´ descendants carried his values in their heart, especially his children. They, together with the Guinness® staff, tried to continue his company in his spirit and as shown before they managed quite well.

We have got the brewery and his values that live on until this day and certainly for many more years. Although he is mostly remembered through his company, he still tried to change the Ireland of his time. "The greatest legacy one can pass on to one's children and grandchildren is not money or other material things accumulated in one's life, but rather a legacy of character and faith." [39], and he did that through the social welfare he participated in, his commitment to the church and a faithful life and simply his idea of a beer that could be good for his people.

---

[37] Irish Pub Operator, North Carolina. „Owner insights ". *The Irish Pub Concept*. The Irish Pub Concept. N.d. Web. 03.11.2016.
[38] Irish Pub Operator, Kansas. „Owner insights ". *The Irish Pub Concept*. The Irish Pub Concept. N.d. Web. 03.11.2016.
[39] BrainyQuote. „Bill Graham Quotes ". *BrainyQuotes*. BrainyQuotes. 2001- 2016. Web. 04.11.2016.

YOUR KNOWLEDGE HAS VALUE

- We will publish your bachelor's and master's thesis, essays and papers

- Your own eBook and book - sold worldwide in all relevant shops

- Earn money with each sale

Upload your text at www.GRIN.com
and publish for free